Jesus is Born

Bibleworld Books contains stories adapted
from the *Contemporary English Version* of the Bible.
Each book is designed to provide early readers with a text
adapted from Scripture in a form and manner that helps them
develop their reading skills and introduce them to the narrative of the Bible.

Adapted from:
Mission Literacy Readers Level 1 & 2
© 2008 American Bible Society
Used by permission.

Jesus is Born is based on Luke 2:1-21

ISBN 978-0-901518-85-9

Series 4: Book 2

Illustrated by Graeme Hewitson

© 2017 The Scottish Bible Society (Formerly The National Bible Society of Scotland).
Company number SC238687, Scottish Charity SC010767
All rights reserved.

SCOTTISH BIBLE SOCIETY
The Word for the world

The Scottish Bible Society
7 Hampton Terrace, Edinburgh. EH12 5XU
www.scottishbiblesociety.org

BIBLEWORLD BOOKS

Series 4: The Story of Jesus' Birth

Mary and the Angel
Jesus is Born

**Bibleworld Books provides three full session outlines
to accompany each story book with games and activities
designed to raise each child's learning potential.**

Available for free download at www.bibleworld.co.uk

A long time ago in Judea,

it was time for Mary's baby to be born.

A law had been made that meant Mary and Joseph had to travel to Bethlehem to be counted by the Romans.

It was a long way, and hard travelling!

When they arrived in Bethlehem, the first thing they did was to go to the inn.

The innkeeper said,

"I'm sorry; all the rooms are taken. But you can stay with the animals, if you like."

After they were inside,

the baby was born.

Mary dressed him, and laid him down in a manger to sleep,

with the animals watching.

That same night, outside the town, under the starry sky,

there were shepherds in the fields with their sheep.

An angel came to them there.
"Don't be afraid," the angel said.

"Rejoice!
The Saviour is born!

You will find him lying in a manger. Go and see him!"

And suddenly angels were all around, singing and praising God!

The shepherds hurried down the road to the town.

They found the place where Mary and Joseph and the baby were staying, and went inside to see them.

They were so happy!
And they went away talking
about what the angel had said.